Lin and Hal

by Linda Johnson
illustrated by Paige Keiser

Core Decodable 15

Mc Graw Hill Education

Bothell, WA • Chicago, IL • Columbus, OH • New York, NY

MHEonline.com

McGraw Hill Education

Copyright © 2015 McGraw-Hill Education

All rights reserved. No part of this publication may be reproduced or distributed in any form or by any means, or stored in a database or retrieval system, without the prior written consent of McGraw-Hill Education, including, but not limited to, network storage or transmission, or broadcast for distance learning.

Send all inquiries to:
McGraw-Hill Education
8787 Orion Place
Columbus, OH 43240

ISBN: 978-0-02-143379-7
MHID: 0-02-143379-8

Printed in the United States of America.

2 3 4 5 6 7 8 9 DOC 20 19 18 17 16 15

Lin had a plan.

Hal can land in sand.

Lin slips in the sand.

Lin sits on a hill.

Hal slips on plants.

Lin and Hal stand still.